THE TRAVELING
TURTLE

G.E. HAWTHORNE

Copyright © 2019 by G.E. Hawthorne

Copyright © 2019 The Traveling Turtle. All rights reserved. No part of this publication may be reproduced, distributed, or transmitted in any form or by any means, including photocopying, recording, or other electronic or mechanical methods, without the prior written permission of the publisher, except in the case of brief quotations embodied in critical reviews and certain other noncommercial uses permitted by copyright law. This also includes conveying via email without permission in writing from the publisher. This book is for entertainment purposes only. All work is fiction creation from the mind of the author, all persons or places relating to real-life characters or locations is purely coincidental.

Dedication

My husband and three sons. Thanks for your unwavering loyalty.
Love You.

It started with a boy named Louis, you see.

He had a terrapin turtle whose name was Benji.

"Guess where we are going?" Louis said in a cheer.

"We are going to Indiana!" the boy shouted clear.

See, Benji's life had started out rather rough.

He used to live by the sea until things turned tough.

The humans chased them away to build a resort instead.

Benji lost everything, his family, friends, and a bed

Benji and his family had nothing happy at all.

They couldn't find food during winter or fall.

Some fell into traps, others got lost in the sun.

Benji hated the humans for what they had done.

Until one day he was so hungry and sad,

He didn't want to continue the life that he had.

Just as he was about to give up and cry,

He heard some footsteps suddenly walk by.

"Louis just look, a turtle in need," a man had said.

That's how Benji found a home, a family, and a bed.

It took a long while, Benji had lost trust.
But each and every day, that coldness started to rust.
Louis played games, and made Benji smile.
They'd laugh together and make jokes for a while.

Louis fed him each day so he could grow strong.
He helped Benji feel like he'd finally belong.
All because Louis showed him great love and care.
Benji loved humans and knew nice ones were there.

Benji laughed as he watched the boy dance all around.

He wanted to dance, but he couldn't get up off the ground

No matter how much he'd try to dance with his friend.

It made Louis smile, so it was worth it in the end.

Before Benji came, Louis learned a lesson or two

About how to care for things smaller than you.

His dad taught him well, how to have a big heart,

And with Benji, it was the perfect place to start.

Every day, Louis would show Benji he cared,

Though his friends and family only just stared.

Even the neighbors didn't know why Louis would try

To care for a turtle that was about to die.

He showed Louis how to care for everyone.

The birds at the park, the cats, a honeybee.

Especially the turtle found alone at the sea.

Once Louis saw the poor turtle in need,

He knew he could help him. That's a true friend indeed.

It was the day at the vet when everything became true.

"He's the healthiest turtle. He's finally pulled through!"

That night Benji and Louis threw a party so fun,

To remember and look back on how far they had come.

Now that brings us to this new adventure today.

"No, no," Dad said. "Benji can't come, it might not be good."

Louis felt so sad. "But you know Benji could!"

Of course, Dad knew the work and time Louis spent.

Now Benji was better, he could go where they went.

They went to Indiana and would it be swell.

They saw the Notre Dame Golden Dome with a view,

Benji couldn't believe all the things he got to do.

It was beautiful and bright, Benji would remember every bit.

Louis carried him when they'd walk and put him down when they'd sit.

Next, they went to the Motor Speedway and watched a 500-mile race.

Benji couldn't believe those cars had such a fast pace.

Benji was a turtle, no way he'd go that fast,

But he got to see the race, and boy, it was a blast!

Next, they went to Lake Michigan where he watched Louis play.

The sky was clear, so he felt the sun's rays.

And every so often Louis would come see

To make sure little Benji was as happy as could be.

Then they went to Virginia. Shenandoah National Park!

Benji had never seen such big trees with bark.

In fact, this was the first forest he'd ever been to.

Thanks to Louis, he's having adventures so new.

Though the best part of all was at Chesapeake Bay.

The water was fresh so Benji could get out and play.

He swam through the water and bit at the leaves,

And he dried in the sun and smelled the fresh trees.

However, what he didn't expect was the next spot.

It was on the other side of the country, they'd traveled a lot.

"Seattle, Washington." Louis gave him a clue,

But Benji had to fly on a plane, he didn't know what to do.

It helped him stay distracted throughout all the plane noise.

As they finally arrived and went to see the great city,

Benji agreed that it was all very pretty.

Queen Anne Hill was the first place, then Beacon Hill.

Then Capitol Hill until they'd all had their fill.

"Wow!" Louis on top of Columbia Center's roof.

It was the tallest building in Seattle, and now they had proof!

It was such a great building; it took his breath away.

Benji could look out forever, he'd be happy to stay.

Yet on to Lake Union they went with such bliss,

There wasn't anything Benji had wanted to miss.

When Louis's arms would grow tired of carrying his friend,

His father would help so Benji could stay till the end.

They reached Gas Works Park and they sat on the ground.

The grass was quite comfy, and the water did astound.

It shimmered and shone like it was made of silver or gold.

They sat there in silence, as the view never got old.

As they packed up once more, it was time to head back.

"Look, Dad! Benji did great!" Louis gave him a snack.

"He sure did," said Dad, for he was awful proud

That his son took such great care of the friend that he'd found.

Benji smiled too, because he felt their love like a fire,

Because Louis gave love that would never expire.

Once they were all back home, Benji was comfy to be
In a house where he learned how to be happy and free.

Football games, video games, playtime, and more.
Benji would be there, that's what best friends were for.

No matter how many years would pass them by,
Benji would be there in the blink of an eye.
Louis grew bigger, taller in size,
But he still loved his Benji, which was no surprise.
To Louis, his turtle was more than a pet.

Throughout the years they'd continue to grow

And spread all the love they had come to show.

Benji and Louis were a wonderful pair.

All it took was patience, teamwork, and care.

The End.

www.ingramcontent.com/pod-product-compliance
Lightning Source LLC
Chambersburg PA
CBHW040759150426
42811CB00055B/1071